YELLOWSTONE
THE GRAND OLD PARK

WILLIAM K. ALMOND

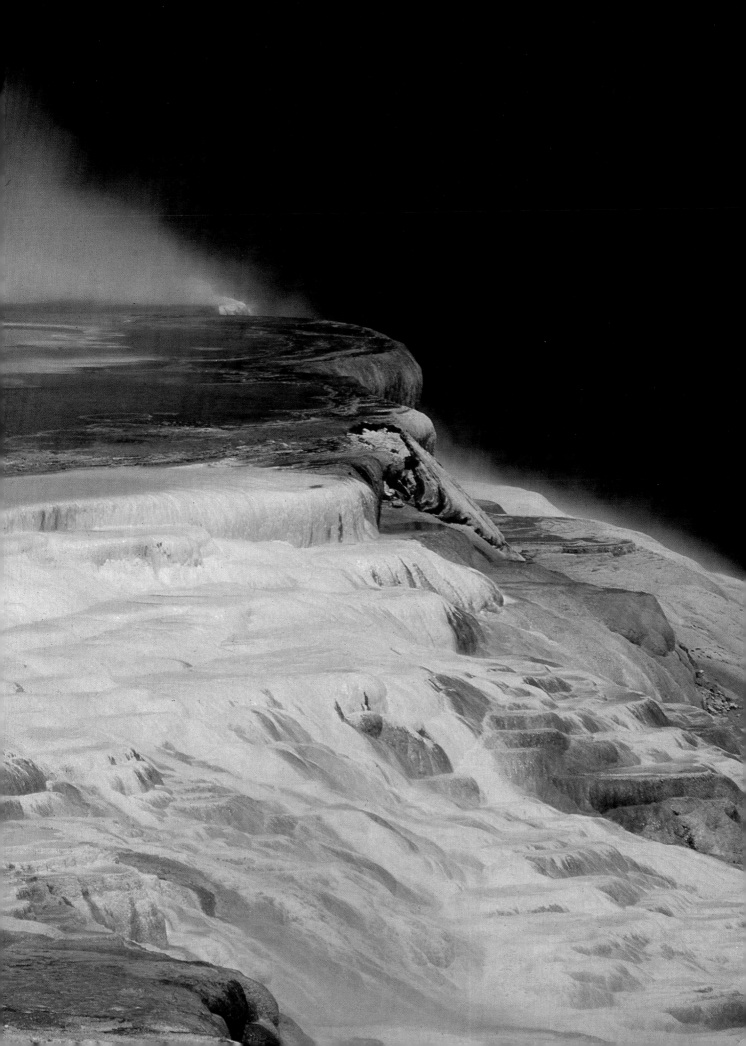

Written, designed and edited
by
Randy Collings

Art and Graphics by
Rick Miller and Roy Murphy

Published for and in behalf of
Yellowstone Park Division
TWA SERVICES, INC.
by
ADAM RANDOLPH COLLINGS

1201 W. Cerritos • P.O. Box 8658, Anaheim, CA 92802

YELLOWSTONE
THE GRAND OLD PARK

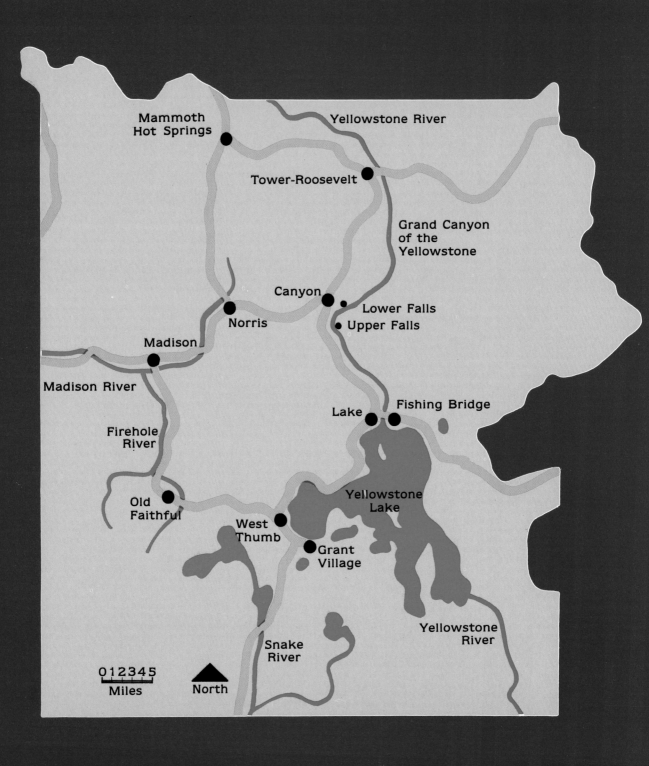

Mammoth Hot Springs

Yellowstone River

Tower-Roosevelt

Grand Canyon of the Yellowstone

Canyon

Lower Falls

Upper Falls

Norris

Madison

Madison River

Firehole River

Fishing Bridge

Lake

Old Faithful

West Thumb

Yellowstone Lake

Grant Village

Snake River

Yellowstone River

0 1 2 3 4 5
Miles

North

YELLOWSTONE
THE GRAND OLD PARK

DISCOVERY: November 1807

SET APART: By an act of Congress on March 1, 1872

LOCATION: Midway between equator and north pole at the 45th parallel in Wyoming's northwest corner. Park boundaries extend into both the state of Montana and the state of Idaho.

SIZE: 2,219,823 acres (roughly the size of Rhode Island and Delaware combined).

DESCRIPTION: A high plateau approximately 7,000 feet in elevation surrounded on all sides by extensions of the Rocky Mountains.

FEATURES: Over 10,000 thermal displays, including Old Faithful (symbol of the Yellowstone), a geyser that has erupted at regular, almost hourly intervals for as long as it has been observed — The Grand Canyon of the Yellowstone River, a magnificent example of the power of erosion at work — Yellowstone Lake, the largest body of water at such a high elevation in North America — and extensive wildlife populations of bison, elk, moose, deer, antelope, bighorn sheep, grizzly and black bear, and many other species.

FLOYD HOLDMAN

THE YELLOWSTONE PARK ACT
Approved March 1, 1872

Be it enacted by the Senate and House of Representatives of the United States of America in Congress assembled, That the tract of land in the Territories of Montana and Wyoming, lying near the headwaters of the Yellowstone river ... is hereby reserved and withdrawn from settlement, and dedicated and set apart as a public park or pleasureing-ground for the benefit and enjoyment of the people.

It was while in the service of a frontier shopkeeper that Virginian frontiersman John Colter gained his place in American history. Working for Lewis and Clark had brought young Colter into the Rocky Mountain territories. He had set out in 1803 to seek his fame and fortune. Miraculously he lived to achieve both. By all standards he should have perished a dozen times due to his own recklessness and perhaps in part to the wild nature of the American frontier.

Nonetheless he survived to be hired on as a salesman in 1807. Manuel Lisa, an enterprising businessman, contracted the intrepid mountain-man to spread the word about his new trading post, Manuel's fort, abroad to Indian nations and trappers within 500 miles of Big Horn River. While so doing in November of that fateful year, Colter stumbled onto the most extensive thermal basin in the world. Dubbed Colter's Hell, few believed the seemingly ridiculous stories of water volcanoes, boiling mud, and mountainous rainbow-colored hot springs that the frontier salesman brought back with him. When Jim Bridger happened upon the same scene several years later, Colter's credibility suffered a further setback. Everyone knew that Bridger could stretch the truth until it vanished. The River that got "heated up" on the bottom; a glass mountain, "peetrified"-trees. Soon no one believed John Colter.

French trappers had christened a high country river that flowed into the Missouri the Roche Jaune, probably because of the yellowish sandstone bluffs characteristic of its riverbanks. To the Crow and Blackfoot, the E-chee-dick-karsh-ah-shay or Elk River had been its name.

With the acquisition of the territory through which it flowed by the United States of America from Napoleon in Thomas Jefferson's famous Louisiana Purchase, the Yankee translation from Roche Jaune to Yellowstone became popular. Through association the name was bestowed upon not only the river itself but the vast Rocky Mountain plateau from which it drained; thus becoming synonymous with the supposedly mythical land of Colter and Bridger's story-telling.

Years passed. The mountain-men and trappers never tired of spinning yarns about the mysterious "Yellow Stone Country." It was not until 1870 that an official government expedition under the auspices of Henry D. Washburn, surveyor general for the State of Montana, set out to determine the veracity of Bridger's "tall-tales." Accompanied by a small military escort, the party made its way into the high country plateaus of nature's most spectacular wonderland. Within a month's time they had vindicated Colter's stories by mapping out such oddities as Mammoth Hot Springs, Old Faithful Geyser, and the spectacular Grand Canyon of the Yellowstone.

Legend had it that one evening, while the expedition camped near the junction of the Gibbon and Firehole rivers, Judge Cornelius Hedges, a member of the party, proposed that rather than attempt to exploit the region, measures should be taken to protect it for the sake of preserving for posterity the incredible sights they had just witnessed.

All in the tiny group agreed. A concept so out of synch with the times, preservation in an era of exploitation, it would take much to convince the people and the Congress of the United States to act upon the far-sighted proposal.

A crusade began. In 1871 a second expedition

was organized; this one equipped with a photographer, William H. Jackson, and an artist, Thomas Moran, to bring back proof of the singular nature and priceless value of this Rocky Mountain wilderness.

When Congress opened session in 1872, each member found placed upon his desk a portfolio of photography and art that must have held the chambers breathless. The proposed law was past, creating Yellowstone National Park, the first reserve of its kind in the world.

This far reaching motion is one of which the American people today are most proud. In a land governed of the people, by the people, and for the people, the people were wise enough to preserve the wild essence of their frontier while the elements were still to be had in abundance. Today when the buffalo has all but become extinct Yellowstone remains as the home of the nation's last significant wild herd. Although trapped out of existence elsewhere throughout the West, beaver still flourish in the streams and rivers of this great national park. Yellowstone is the last major stronghold outside of Alaska for the noble American grizzly and while elk population have dwindled or vanished elsewhere, here on these high country plateaus roam the largest elk herds in the United States.

Because of the foresight of a small group of men sensitive to the value of wilderness, all Americans are able to experience in the Yellowstone the abundance and beauty of a frontier long since vanished elsewhere.

At the North entrance to this Grand Old Park, inscribed on a stone arch, are the words that define most appropriately the philosophy of the National Park system. It reads: "For the benefit and enjoyment of the people."

Henry D. Washburn
1869

Fascinated by tales of Colter's Hell, visitors from then until now have flocked to this Rocky Mountain "wonderland." Some come to satisfy curiosity; others to worship and reflect.

Today Yellowstone plays host to more than 2.5 million guests a year. All are served by the attentive National Park Service employees and gracious hospitality of both TWA and Hamilton Stores, Inc. (concessionnaires to The Grand Old Park).

Early postcards of the Yellowstone, courtesy of Hamilton Stores, Inc.

Beginning with the Washburn expedition of 1870 and continuing on to the present, scientist from virtually every field have studied the Yellowstone seeking for origins. Much has been learned.

Geologists have determined that several hundred million years ago this entire region lay beneath the waters of a warm shallow sea. Hundreds of feet of limestone created by the fossilized bodies of tiny sea creatures bare witness to their one time abundance. About 100 million years ago the waters of the sea abated. Great marshlands remained, providing feeding grounds for the mighty dinosaurs. Giant Brontosaurus and Tyrannosaurus Rex thundered over these lands.

The waters continued to receed. Marshes disappeared and with them vanished the giant reptiles. Subtropical environs gave way to forests of pine and fir. The mighty sequoia redwood, found today only in California's Sierra Nevada Mountains, flourished here in the Yellowstone.

Then suddenly, several hundred thousand years ago, the horizon burst into flames. Continental plates shifting eastward from the Pacific buckled and warped beneath the earth's surface, releasing molten lava from below. This mountain building activity gave birth to the Gallatin, Beartooth, and Teton Ranges and accounts for their jagged peaks and rugged complexion. Violent volcanic activity buried the rich timberlands of the Yellowstone plateau beneath a blanket of ash. Eventually the forests grew back only to be destroyed again by further volcanic activity. These processes repeated themselves 27 times. They account for the odd petrified trees and extensive geyser activity scattered throughout the region today.

Volcanic activity still threatens. Hot molten lava near the surface heats the crystal clear springs of this Western wilderness, sending them skyward in beautiful thermal displays that delight the senses. Yet it is precisely this activity that has brought about the fiery destruction of these forest lands time and time again. One can only speculate that either the geyser's themselves will gradually cease to exist or that the area will again errupt and spill forth a blanket of ash and destruction. Such processes however run their course over periods of time so vast that, to our finite mortal state, we ought best to realize it most unlikely that you or I will live to see either possibly occur.

———————

To experience Yellowstone is to awaken the senses of the inner being. John Muir, one of America's most beloved naturalists, once stated that in returning to such country as that of this great national park, we almost feel as if we are coming home. Park employees find this sentiment expressed in another way on the wall of their orientation hall. Quoting Arapooish, a Crow Indian Chief, the inscription reads: "Yellowstone . . . is a good country. The Great Spirit has put it exactly in the right place, while you are in it you fare well."

PHOTOGRAPHS: US NATIONAL PARK SERVICE

FOR THE BENEFIT AND
ENJOYMENT OF THE PEOPLE

YELLOWSTONE
NATIONAL
PARK

At Gardiner, Montana, stately Theodore Roosevelt arch (previous page) spans the highway, serving as an official gateway to nature's wonderland. The more than 2.5 million visitors who pass through it or any of four other portals to the Yellowstone are rewarded with a view of pristine wilderness.

Aside from her world famous natural wonders, Yellowstone National Park is "the American West" as it was a century ago — unspoiled and abounding in wildlife. Rocky Mountain Bighorn Sheep (right and below) roam the highlands and Pronghorn antelope (previous page) are frequently seen in the northern reaches of the Park.

Here in this great reserve the American Bison (below right) or buffalo, symbol of a nation's legendary frontier, is still today a common sight.

PHOTOGRAPHS: US NATIONAL PARK SERVICE

FLOYD HOLDMAN

Spectacular Mammoth Hot Springs (previous page and these pages) is unequaled in both size and beauty by any other thermal springs in the world. It has been estimated that each day nearly two tons of dissolved limestone is carried by over 500 gallons of water per minute over the pastel-colored stairways that flank mighty Terrace Mountain.

At the base of this vast phenomenon stands 37-foot-high Liberty Cap (left) an unusual cone composed of calcium carborate, mineral deposited in days past when hot water flowed from its orifice at the top.

Just beyond Mammoth Hot Springs stands Roosevelt Lodge, an ideal basecamp from which to enjoy all the pleasures of Yellowstone's great western playground.

Horseback riding, chuck wagon-style dinners and even an authentic Yellowstone Transportation Company Stage Coach delight Park visitors of all ages.

Second only to the Yellowstone's spectacular thermal displays, this region's countless specimens of petrified trees tell of an ancient past when violent volcanic activity buried these rich timberlands beneath blankets of ash.

At Tower Falls (right) further evidence of this repeated volcanic action is displayed as extensive "columnar jointing," rows of basaltic lava, that line the surrounding canyon walls (below).

PHOTOGRAPHS: WILLIAM K. ALMOND

RALPH L. HOPKINS

Sixty foot Undine Falls (far left) plummets between perpendicular canyon walls along lava creek.

Summer here in the high country is short, yet incredibly beautiful. For a few brief months wildflower displays (left) grace meadows and grasslands.

Ursus Americanus, the American black bear (below) comes out of his winter hibernation to indulge in the short-lived season's abundance of sunshine and sustenance.

WILLIAM K. ALMOND

PHOTOGRAPHS: US NATIONAL PARK SERVICE

Unlike cousin black bear, Ursus horribilis or American Grizzly (previous page and these pages), much as his name would imply, demands the ultimate respect (some would call it fear) from intruders in his world. Yellowstone is one of the last major strongholds of this most noble of North American wildlife. Averaging some 300 to 600 pounds at maturity, the Grizzly prefers Yellowstone's back country. There he roams as monarch of the wilderness.

44

PHOTOGRAPHS: US NATIONAL PARK SERVICE

The awesome beauty of Yellowstone's Grand Canyon (these pages and following pages) has captured the hearts of painters, photographers, and poets alike.

A supreme example of the power of erosion, here the Yellowstone River roars over two mighty falls and golden-colored gorges along a 24-mile course of unparalleled scenic grandeur.

Boasting the largest population of elk in the world, Yellowstone's mighty Wapiti (these pages and following pages) are among the largest of the deer family. Mature bulls may weigh upwards of 900 lbs. and form an awesome sight in late summer and early fall when their annual display of antlers reach the measure of their expansion.

ALAN CAREY

Yellowstone Lake's one hundred mile shoreline affords scenic waterfront as well as limitless recreational opportunities. Fishing Bridge (above) is a popular place for anglers while sunworshipers enjoy any of several sparkling beaches (right). Beautiful Lake Hotel (above right) offers the finest in resort accommodations.

TWA SERVICES

US NATIONAL PARK SERVICE

The largest high elevation body of water in North America, Yellowstone Lake (below) at 7,733 ft. above sea level stretches 20 miles long and 14 miles wide. *Bridge Bay Marina* (below right) offers complete boating facilities for those who wish to venture out into the lake's sparkling blue expanse.

Canadian Geese (right) spend their summers here on the Yellowstone before seeking warmer climes during winters.

WILLIAM K. ALMOND

US NATIONAL PARK SERVICE

ED COOPER

Grand Prismatic Spring (above) near Yellowstone's Midway Geyser basin (previous page) is one of the largest and by far among the most beautiful of any such hotspring in the Park. Ideal for growing algae, the spring's heated water gives rise to brilliant displays of yellow, orange, green and gold growth.

Elsewhere Firehole Springs cause the temperature of the famous Firehole River to rise; hence, Bridger's "River that gets heated up on the bottom," is not really caused by friction as the mountain man supposed, but rather due to the abundant influx of hot water from geyser basins and thermal hot springs such as these along the river's course.

ED COOPER

FLOYD HOLDMAN

FLOYD HOLDMAN

Riverside Geyser, most picturesque in the park (above and left) erupts every 5½ to 8 hours. For twenty minutes she sends forth a 75 foot column of water that gracefully arches over the Firehole River. Elsewhere constant variation in the flow of thermal hot springs terminates once flourishing stands of pine (above left).

PHOTOGRAPHS: DANNY FELD

The peculiar shape and unusual reflective qualities of Morning Glory Pool (above and above right) have given this beautiful hot spring its sobriquet. Like the flower whose name it bares, the inner chamber of this colorful fountain throws back to the eye the deepest blue of the sky above.

Elsewhere throughout the Park hundreds of thermal displays (right) abound.

Within the Yellowstone are more thermal features than exist altogether elsewhere throughout the world. More than 10,000 such hot springs, fumaroles, mud pots and geysers are concentrated primarily within six major basins.

*oiling mud at Black Dragon's Caldron (r*ight) and Fountain Paint Points (left) *b*ubble and gurgle like thick, murky soup. *c*reated by hot springs unable to produce *e*nough moisture to wash away the min*er*al they carry to their surface, these curi*os*ities in such profusion are found no*w*here else in the world.

By far the most spectacular of thermal features in the Yellowstone, are the geysers. Some 300 of them delight park visitors with their thrilling displays of boiling water and steam. Water volcanos (right) will erupt at intervals ranging from every few minutes, or even constantly, to once every decade. Some displays are brief while others like that of Grotto Geyser (below) may continue for hours.

US NATIONAL PARK SERVICE

ED COOPER

The spectacle of Old Faithful's hourly eruption embodies the very spirit of wildness. Unharnessed energy shoots nearly two hundred feet of boiling water skyward as clouds of steam billow even higher. Standing like a sentinel overlooking vast thermal geyser basins, Old Faithful has become a world symbol for the preservation of wilderness and promulgation of the national park concept to all countries throughout the world.

TWA GUEST SERVICES

U.S. NATIONAL PARK SERVICE

Historic Old Faithful Lodge and the magnificient Inn (left) offer true rustic grandeur that can only be described as unique. Activities centered around the Upper Geyser Basin include an outstanding visitors center and daily ranger-conducted interpretive programs.

WILLIAM K. ALMOND

To experience Winter in the Yellowstone is
to encounter Yellowstone at its finest.
Freezing temperatures turn geyser displays into billowing clouds of steam that
ascend hundreds of feet into the air. Thermal features abate snow drifts forming
ideal grazing areas for herds of bison and
elk. Wonderland truly appears as just that,
welcoming those willing to brave the chill
to a season of comparative tranquility and
solitude.

US NATIONAL PARK SERVICE

WILLIAM K. ALMOND

THE END

Published for and in behalf of
YELLOWSTONE PARK DIVISION
TWA SERVICES, INC.
Yellowstone National Park, Wyoming 82190